RETHINK EVERYTHING

MIKE PALLIN

Cover by Ric Dominic Zarate
Layout by Princess Hannah Arsenio

RETHINK
EVERYTHING

MIKE PALLIN

Copyright © 2024 by Michael Pallin

Visit the author's website at www.floydwickman.com

All rights reserved. No portion of this book may be reproduced in any form without written permission from the publisher or author, except as permitted by U.S. copyright law.
For permission requests, contact the publisher at: mike@floydwickman.com.

Book Cover by Ric Dominic Zarate

Layout by Princess Hannah Arsenio

First edition: 2024

Dedicated to Mary,
always.

CONTENTS

Foreword xi

Introduction xv

Chapter 1: Listings Are The Name Of The Game 19

Chapter 2: CPR (Close Personal Relationships) 27

Chapter 3: One Stop Shopping 31

Chapter 4: Build An Exit Strategy 34

Chapter 5: Who Do You Know?
And Who Do They Know? 41

Chapter 6: The 5 Biggest Mistakes Real Estate Salespeople Make And How To Avoid Them 49

Chapter 7: It's Not The Calls You Make.
It's That You Make The Calls. 55

Chapter 8: How To Make Yourself Make More Calls
With The 5-90-10 System 59

Chapter 9: How To Generate Your Own Leads
Without Having To Pay For Them 65

Chapter 10: How To Convert Leads Into
Appointments 69

CONTENTS

Chapter 11: The Pricing Presentation 79

Chapter 12: How To Handle Hesitations 85

Chapter 13: Client Appreciation Events
That Pay Off 93

Chapter 14: Finding Off-Market Properties 99

Chapter 15: Train The Brain 105

Chapter 16: Create Accountability 113

Foreword

In 2023, I was invited to speak at an event for The Floyd Wickman Team.

I'd spoken at dozens of coaching events and wasn't sure what to expect.

I met a gentleman who's been in the real estate industry for decades.

I watched him speak; he was brilliant.
I watched him encourage people; he was sincere.
I watched him correct people; he was gracious.

I then watched him pick up an acoustic guitar and play and sing. It was beautiful.

I sat there thinking, "Who is this guy?"

Why had I not heard of him? All my years in the real estate industry, not a peep?

It's because he's not about himself. He's spent years and years in the shadows, making Realtors' lives better and never trying to take any credit.

Well, guess what?!

That changes now!

If you don't know him, I would be honored to introduce you to Mike Pallin!

In 2009, Mike created the R Squared Coaching Program, and since then, year after year, the agents he coaches have produced an average of one listing or sale per person per week.

This man has done it all!

Except…write a book!

You're going to love this book.
You're going to love Mike's advice.
You're going to fall in love with Mike's heart.

Thank you for picking up the third book in the Rethink Everything series, "Rethink Everything You Know About Selling Real Estate." Your life and business will improve if you do what these pages say. I guarantee it!

Love you, Mike! Thanks for taking us on a "Rethink Everything journey!

KYLE DRAPER

INTRODUCTION

If you have a role in the real estate business – whether it's as salesperson, broker, manager, owner, team lead, recruiter, assistant, administrator, trainer, coach, or in one of the many businesses that support the industry – this book is dedicated to you, with gratitude.

And it is specifically written for you if you are just getting started (or restarted) as a salesperson. It has been my good fortune to be mentored by, and partnered with, one of the great original thinkers in real estate, Floyd Wickman. Hundreds of thousands of agents (and their families) are grateful for the influence Floyd's training has had on their careers and their lives.

In all the years of The Floyd Wickman Team working with our clients and their salespeople and observing this industry, two things have become very clear.

#1 The real estate market, like all financial markets, has a tendency to go up and down and up and down. It's always been that way and it will always be that way. As the market goes up and down, so does the population of agents.

#2 Out of every ten people who get into this business, 1 gets to great, 2 get to good, and 7 never make it

Rethink Everything

past licensee. In other words, 70% of the people who get into this business end up leaving before they get anywhere near what they had hoped for and dreamed about.

The most successful people in real estate come in all different shapes and sizes. They have only two traits in common: a willingness to work and teachability. Those who are continuously getting educated, and applying what they learn, give themselves a huge advantage.

If you are new, your greatest assets are time, energy and the enthusiasm that comes with being new. Your greatest weaknesses are doubts, fears and worries. This book is chock full of OPE (other people's experience), the kind that will banish all your doubts, fears and worries. The blueprint in this book is distilled from decades of developing successful and productive real estate salespeople. If our history has taught me anything, it is that you have what it takes to become one of them.

—Mike Pallin

"Buyers provide you with a paycheck. Listings give you a business."

CHAPTER 1:
Listings Are The Name of The Game

"Buyers provide you with a paycheck. Listings give you a business."

Here are ten good reasons why it's vital that you become a skilled listing agent and avoid having to work with buyers.

#1 You are in control of your income in any market.

(No matter what the Department of Justice rules about decoupling commissions, no matter what your state legislature mandates, or your Multiple Listing System requires, sellers have been paying full commission to real estate agents for over 100 years. In fact, the percentage of sales by owner without an has been shrinking steadily this century to less than 5% of the total number of transactions.

#2 You determine your income level.
In other words, if you want a raise all you have to do is get more listings.

#3 In a balanced market, it takes 50% less time and effort to obtain, sell, and close a listing than it does to get a buyer to the closing table.
In an unbalanced market with a less than normal supply of listings, buyers take even longer.

#4 There is far less competition for listings.
Most agents are not proficient at presenting their company's marketing, pricing, and handling hesitations. That means there is less competition. Being a listing agent requires a different set of skills using a lot of logic, and very little emotion. On the other hand, working with buyers requires a lot of emotion and a little logic.

#5 When you have an inventory of listings, all of the other agents are working for you.
Hypothetically, if you had ALL the listings, what percent of the closings would you be involved in? That's right…all of them.

#6 Listing agents are in better control of offers and the follow up to the sale.
The #1 cause of transactions falling through are untrained agents with limited experience and limited control of their clients..

#7 Listing agents are more likely to discover investment opportunities.
Some of our students use Cash For Property ads to generate leads. While sellers will not usually agree to consider an investor price (traditionally between 70% and 75% of market value) they will, which puts you in a perfect position to acquire an investment property. Buy real estate because it's what you know.

#8 Sellers whose home you have sold are the most motivated and competitive buyers.
In fact, in most markets the listings you get will provide you with most, if not all, the buyers you will ever need.

#9 Your listings sell even when you are on vacation or taking a day off.

#10 You may be allowed to sell your own listings thereby doubling your income for a single transaction.

Historically, 7% of listings are sold by the listing agent. With new rules and regulations about agency, it is becoming more common for unrepresented buyers to contact the listing agent directly.

> **Example:** Vicki, one of my coaching students from Texas, listed a $2.5 million dollar ranch. She drove to the adjoining ranch, spoke with the owner to let him know the ranch next door was for sale. He hired Vicki and made a full price offer that was accepted.

> **Example:** Another one of our best students began his career as a successful commercial real estate agent in upstate New York. When the market crashed in 2008 and commercial credit disappeared, he had to reinvent himself as a residential agent. He called Floyd asking for help and direction, "How do I get off to the best start as a residential agent?"

"Oh, I have the perfect answer for what you need to do. But first, go get six listings and then call me back." For the first time in his career, he worked and worked and worked on getting residential listings, and in a month managed to get his six. "Okay, Floyd, I've done everything you asked me to, now how do I get off to the best start as a residential agent?" Floyd said, "Go get six more listings." And Bob has never looked back.

In fact, in 2014, Bob's wife, Debbie, a very well-respected scientist, was offered a position in North Carolina. They moved the family lock, stock and barrel to a town where Bob knew absolutely no one and had to start his real estate business over from scratch. No worries. In the first year, Bob listed 78 properties, all of them from expired listings. His business today is 80% repeat and referrals. If you list, you last.

Yeah, but...

What if my listings don't sell and I have disappointed and upset clients? Remember this – there's nothing wrong with any listing that the right price and terms won't cure. At the time of listing, remind your sellers that you know your marketing works, all we are testing is the price. The market will tell us whether or not we are priced right. Ask them, "How long are you willing to go without getting an offer before we adjust the price?" And then structure built-in price reductions accordingly.

THE FORMULA FOR A GOOD WEEK

"Starting every Monday work on bringing in a saleable listing first." Real estate is an inventory business. When you are out of inventory, you are out of business.

Here's a warning. When you prospect for listings you will experience rejection.

"Have you thought about selling your house?"
"No."
"Have you thought about selling your house?"
"No."
"Have you thought about selling your house?"
"No."

After enough of this rejection, your attitude can become, "You probably don't want to sell your house either, do you?" And that's when the temptation to work with buyers will tug at your sleeve. Especially when they call you and say they want to go look at a house. "Somebody needs me! Finally!"

Don't give in. Don't drop everything you're doing and change direction. Make a commitment to stick with listings until you become competent, confident and natural. Remind yourself of these 10 reasons why listings are the name of the game. The vast majority of long-term successful agents are listing agents, and they are never unemployed.

Building a listing inventory will generate all the buyers you need. Some are drawn to you via marketing efforts, and some will be your sellers who also want to buy. That's why it's imperative to develop powerful presentation skills that showcase your services and demonstrate your value as both a listing agent and a selling agent.

CHAPTER 2:
CPR
(Close Personal Relationships)

Surviving into the future in real estate, and thriving in that future, will depend in large part on your ability to build a business based on repeat clients who also refer you. It all begins with building close personal relationships with clients, and prospects who become your clients.

By the way, a client is someone who will work with you, your way, and not fight you. Clients are people who know you, like you, trust you and respect you. Clients are the difference between a relationship-based business and a transaction-based business. And the #1 benefit of a relationship-based business is that you don't have to start over from scratch every January 1st.

We call this building a "Book of Business," and define it as close personal relationships with up to 200 individuals or families who think of you as "My Realtor®", and think of you whenever they have a conversation with someone they know and the subject of real estate comes up. They happily connect you with their friends, family, neighbors and co-workers – not as a favor to you, but as a favor to them.

Why 200? Sociologists tell us that 200 is the maximum number of intimate, family-type relationships a person can maintain at any one time. Technology, CRMs and social media can connect us to thousands of people, but those connections aren't as close or personal.

These close personal relationships can be created with a consistent marketing program that includes making impressions by sending them something every month; getting voice-to-voice at least three times a year; and seeing them in person at least once a year, supplemented with social media interactions – liking, commenting and sharing. The more you know about what's happening in the lives of the people in your Book of Business, the more personal your interactions become. There is just no substitute for keeping in touch, and showing people that you care about things they care about.

"People don't care what you know until they know that you care."

If you are worried about "pestering" the people you know with multiple calls per year, then just call to check in. Chances are that whenever you check in with someone in your Book of Business, they will ask you about real estate – and that is when you can ask for their help in expanding your business with referrals; when you can reassure them with a promise to serve without pressure; and when you can remind them of who you're looking for (your ideal client).

"I am expanding my business and could really use your help. If I asked you to, would you be willing to refer me to a friend or family member with a real estate need?"

"Let me reassure that when you do I will treat them like they were my own family. I'll never put any pressure on them, and always keep you informed so there's no surprises. Fair enough?"

"I'm especially looking for people who own a home here in our town, and the home has become too much to handle, or too small for their growing family. Who do you know that might fit into either of those situations?"

The 80/20 Rule

Out of your 200 best relationships, in any given year about 20% of them (40 people) will do business with you again or refer someone to you. And an even smaller group within that 20%, your biggest fans and supporters, will refer you multiple times per year. Consistent, personal contacts and engagement should result in a minimum of 24 closings a year, as it has for thousands of our students within their first year of Book of Business building.

The internet has made it possible for buyers to shop for houses online. Selling prospects shop, too, for their listing agent. They visit open houses; they check Google reviews; they join Facebook groups; and they ask their friends, family, neighbors and coworkers for recommendations. Google reviews, social media and open house will get you in front of those shoppers. But building close personal relationships with your clients and prospects will put you top of mind and first in line.

CHAPTER 3:
One Stop Shopping

No one admits to shopping at WalMart, but their stores do have a whopping market share of retail and groceries. Why? They are not always the cleanest on the block, or the friendliest or even offer the greatest selection. People shop WalMart because everything is under one roof. It's one stop shopping. Convenience is the key.

The idea behind being able to offer one stop shopping to your clients is to keep you, the real estate agent, at the center of the transaction.

In addition to building close personal relationships with your clients and prospects, build relationships with your vendor partners – all those people and businesses that serve the real estate consumer. Your clients are looking for your recommendations and guidance throughout the transaction and beyond.

When you can become a go-to source for reliable, affordable, friendly, quality services and service people, you are on your way to offering one stop shopping.

You probably have a favorite loan officer, title officer, warranty company, inspector, and appraiser. Expand your vendor partner list to include people you trust to deliver timely, world-class service. Consider creating a "yellow pages" style directory to help promote their business. Invite them to your client appreciation events. Get your vendor partners together for their own appreciation and networking event a la BNI, Business Networking International.

Spotlight local businesses and their owners on your social media platforms. And pay special attention to those people in your Book of Business who own and operate their own business. Your vendor partners and business owners can become an additional source of referrals.

5 QUESTIONS

Here's how to approach business owners to establish a referral relationship. When you offer to help them with their business before asking them to refer you, your odds soar that they will be receptive to the idea. Use each of these questions as a conversation starter.

1. *Do you accept referrals in your business?*
2. *Who is your ideal client (or best customer)?*
3. *When I run across someone like that in my real estate business, what would you like me to say about you? (your elevator speech)*
4. *How would you like me to connect you with them?*
5. *Would you be open to trading referrals?*

In most cases, you bring the client to the transaction. Not the mortgage, insurance, or title person. You are giving them access to your clients, and they are making a nice living from your referrals. Let them know they can count on you, and that you count on them. When you do, they will go out of their way to help you and your clients safely across the finish line.

Rethink Everything

CHAPTER 4:
Building An Exit Strategy

Hey, wait a minute. I just got here, and you want me to think about leaving the business?

In a word, yes. As Warren Buffet's partner, Charlie Munger, always advised, "Begin with the end in mind." So, I want you to think about how and when you want to leave real estate.

Some people never quit. Some never even slow down. One of the agents I coach is in her mid 60's, in the business 40 years, and has been asked many times when she is going to retire. Her answer is one of my favorite lines. She says, "Well, my mother is 84 and she is still selling full time. When she retires, I'll think about it." As long as you love doing what you're doing, it's never work.

But there is no gold watch, 401K pension and retirement village condo for most real estate agents. If there comes a time when you cannot work, or don't want to work anymore, how do you fund a retirement from real estate? Is there a way to get to the point where you only work because you want to, and not because you have to?

There are lots of retirement plans and investments that might eventually give you the choice of freedom from having to work, but there are two in particular that you can count on. "Building a saleable Book of Business and buying real estate, and let's take them one at a time.

SALEABLE BOOK OF BUSINESS

In the financial-services world they call it continuity of practice. Professionals who develop fiduciary relationships with a client base want their clients to be taken care of after they retire, so they take great care in selecting and developing the right person to "continue" their business. They either sell the business for a lump sum, or a series of payments based on performance. Very often they hire a business broker to put the sale together.

This has also been happening in the real estate world, especially on the brokerage level through mergers and acquisitions, though not so much on the agent level. Unfortunately, most agents never build the components of a business that make it saleable: data, systems and history. And one more very important ingredient, profitability.

DATA

There's no substitute for information. It is the age we live in. The more information you can collect about the people in your Book of Business (your 200 best repeat and referral business sources) the more you can personalize your marketing and deepen your clients' loyalty. This is more than a list of cell phone numbers and email addresses. The data includes children's names, pet's names, birthdays, hobbies, vacation destinations, etc. This is the kind of information that friends and families share with one another, and that's who you must become. The piece that's often missing is the ability to keep this data in a retrievable place so you don't forget it, and so it can be easily transferred to someone else when the time is right.

SYSTEMS

If technology has made real estate easier in any way, it is with systemizing processes: data input, activity tracking, accounting, client follow up, prospecting, contract preparation, and closing work. The best kind of business is the kind that's working even when you're not. Systems make that possible.

HISTORY

Once your Book of Business is operating consistently over time, you create measurable value – something worth selling, and something worth paying for. Your business history will show your operating expenses, commission income and the difference between the two, or profit. If someone were to purchase your business, mine the data you've collected and adopt your systems, they should be able to earn what you can prove you've been earning. That's the power of history, and it's how you will determine the value of your business when it's time to sell it.

BUY REAL ESTATE

You may be a financial wizard. You may be a can't miss stock picker. A wildly successful day trader. An online poker champion. There are so many ways to become financially secure and independent, yet most of them depend on specialized knowledge and skill (along with some luck.) It usually boils down to what you know and what you're good at.

You know real estate. You're good at it. So you should invest in real estate. It is one of the very few dependable appreciating assets. And as a listing agent, over the course of your career, you will be presented with opportunities to buy low and sell high. That is, when you learn and use the Wickman pricing presentation, which begins something like this…

"NAME and NAME Seller, as you know, there are three prices on every house. There is wholesale, the price an investor would pay you; not to live in it, but to resell it for profit. And there is retail. That's the price John and Jane Doe would pay to live here. And the third price on every house is your list price; and your price is determined by one factor, time.

"Let's take wholesale. If an investor made you an offer, they would factor in buying, selling and holding costs, and then profit, so they'd probably come in somewhere in the neighborhood of 70% of retail, or in your case, oh... (and here you name a figure you have calculated at 70% of full market value).

"You know, I just had a thought. What if I could get you that much, all cash, and it only took a day or two. Would you even consider it?"

Almost all of the time, your client will say, "No way." And you will say, "I don't blame you, I wouldn't either."

But every once in a while, especially if you go on 50 or more listing appointments a year, they will say, "You know, we might. What would that look like?" And that's when preparation meets opportunity. Pull up your purchase contract and start filling it out.

It will be to your great advantage to develop investor clients and sources of funds to help you buy real estate when presented with an opportunity.

In combination, passive income from a saleable Book of Business and cash flow from a real estate portfolio can make for a very comfortable retirement. As exit strategies go, this combo has two very important ingredients to recommend it. First, when you invest in real estate, you are investing in a commodity you know a great deal about. And second, when you transfer your business to the right person, your clients will be well taken care of.

CHAPTER 5:
Who Do You Know?
And Who Do They Know?

In every Floyd Wickman Program we give our students an exercise during the first session called the Who Do You Know Who? List (see figure 5-1). There are 101 categories of people (family, friends, neighbors, church, dry cleaners, etc.) with instructions to estimate how many people in each category they could contact and how many of those might be candidates for their Book of Business. To graduate they are required to have 200 candidates on their list and to have already sent them something. To some of our students, especially the new agents, it seems impossible…until they do the exercise, and realize – "Hey, I know more people than I thought I did. Coming up with 200 is going to be easier than I

Rethink Everything

thought!" Which is, of course, why we do the exercise the first day.

We had a student who started the program the same week she moved to the market area from out of state to live with her aunt. She knew nobody locally, so she borrowed her aunt's address book and started calling people who knew her aunt. She generated 37 referral leads in 42 days.

You probably know more people than you think you do, so build a healthy repeat and referral-based business with them. Do the math. If you know 200 people, and they each know 200 people – that's 40,000 people. People they are connected with, people they see and talk with regularly, people they work with, people they go to church with, etc. And that's the point of building "relational equity" with your favorite 200, because when you do, the people you know will give you access to the people they know.

If you really do not know 200 people and you don't have an aunt that does, you still need 200 on your list. Not only do you now realize that you are sadly lacking in acquaintances, but you can make a commitment to start meeting more people, being more friendly, and having more conversations. You might consider adding all your neighbors (and then working at getting to know them) or all the parents of your third grader's classroom friends. You could start a new hobby like pickleball or golf. The secret is to find something that you like doing so you stay involved with the people you meet.

The 200 you start with isn't the 200 you end with. Some will have a Realtor already, some won't like you, some will move away. Those folks go off the list when you find someone to add who is willing to send you referrals.

Mail, call, see and engage. Send them something every month. Call them three times a year. Get together with them in person once a year. And engage with them on social media.

Repetitive contacts with the people you know make you memorable. In survey after survey of consumers, 86% of those who buy a house say they will use the same agent who represented them in the purchase when it is time to sell. Only 14% actually do, in large part because their agent didn't stay in touch after the sale.

"More business is lost due to a lack of consistent follow-up than for any other reason."

Rethink Everything

Instructions:

Write down the number of people you could contact in the far-left column under the # sign. In the second column, marked P, estimate the number who could be Platinum B.O.B. candidates. Total the columns.

B	P	
		1. Your family
		2. Your partner's family
		3. Your "extended" family
		4. Your acquaintances
		5. Your partner's acquaintances
		6. Your best friends
		7. Your partner's best friends
		8. Children's friends and parents
		9. Children's teachers, coaches, etc
		10. Dentist, orthodontist, optometrist, etc.
		11. Doctors / chiropractors / health practitioners
		12. Yoga, Pilates, Health Club, YMCA, etc.
		13. Hairdressers/barbers
		14. Dry cleaning / laundry
		15. Pedicures, manicures, facials, masseuse, etc.
		16. Social media friends, connections, subscribers, followers
		17. Internet leads
		18. Services your car, sells you gas, tires, etc.
		19. Sold you your current car
		20. Sold you cars in the past
		21. Delivers your mail
		22. Place of worship
		23. At the convenience store
		TOTALS

B	P	
		24. At the grocery store
		25. At the pharmacy
		26. Owes you money
		27. At the bank
		28. Stock broker
		29. Financial planner
		30. Prepares your taxes
		31. Does your accounting
		32. Veterinarian
		33. Pet Care
		34. Your favorite restaurants
		35. Favorite bartender
		36. Country club / tennis club / health spa
		37. Children's sporting events
		38. Go to concerts with
		39. Go to the movies with
		40. Go to other cultural events or places with
		41. Go on vacations with
		42. See only once or twice a year
		43. Go to breakfast with
		44. Your attorney
		45. In the trades: furnace, A/C, plumbing, roofing
		46. Pest control
		47. Fix your roof / electrical problem
		48. Built your deck
		49. Picks up your trash
		50. Runs your neighborhood / condo association
		51. Fed Ex / UPS person
		52. Mows your lawn, lears your driveway
		TOTALS

B	P	
		53. Landscaping
		54. Built your house
		55. Landlord
		56. Insurance agents
		57. Sells you clothing
		58. Tailor / seamstress / dressmaker
		59. Sells you make-up / supplements / vitamins
		60. In a multi-level marketing organization
		61. Sells you computers
		62. Fixes your computer
		63. Travel agent
		64. Printer
		65. Receive holiday cards from
		66. Send holiday cards to
		67. Buy furniture from
		68. Arts and crafts
		69. Office supplies
		70. You see at your office building
		71. Sells you meat / seafood
		72. Hardware store
		73. At the library
		74. In law enforcement
		75. In politics
		76. You have done business with
		77. Service and fraternal organizations
		78. Social organizations
		79. Industry and trade organizations
		80. Sells you carpets, drapes, appliances
		81. Education and military network
		TOTALS

B	P	
		82. Florist
		83. Neighbors
		84. Hobby supplies
		85. Jeweler
		86. Photographer
		87. Previous neighbors
		88. Day care centers / nursery schools / pre-K
		89. Spouse or parents' sphere of influence
		90. Buy advertising from
		91. Suppliers and vendors at work
		92. Currently trying to sell you something
		93. Presides at a religious/spiritual ceremony
		94. Delivers your water / water softener supplies
		95. Sells shoes to you
		96. Maintains your security system
		97. Handles your communications equipment
		98. Play cards/bowl with
		99. Investors
		100. Rental agencies
		101. Asset managers for REO, HUD, FNMA, VA
		TOTALS
		TOTALS from page 44
		TOTALS from page 45
		TOTALS from page 46
		GRAND TOTALS
		TOTALS

Rethink Everything

CHAPTER 6:
The 5 Biggest Mistakes Real Estate Salespeople Make And How To Avoid Them

With over 1.6 million agents in North America, you can bet there are a lot of mistakes made. Unfortunately, selling real estate isn't like cutting hair. If it were, an agent would have practiced writing contracts for dozens of people, over many months with a supervisor's observation and input. In real estate, a new agent is lucky to have a mentor or a manager that knows their name. It's rare that anyone attends an agent's first appointments. Even if they did a "sample contract" once or twice in a classroom, most write a real contract for the first time when they have a live Buyer or Seller. It's no wonder 70% fail in their first two years.

Many who do stay in the business earn a paltry sum. They just can't seem to get it together and while they may be nice people and know what to do with a contract, they spend a lot of time working with folks who never buy or sell with them.

What a tragedy.

What if you could beat the odds and become successful? Here are the five biggest mistakes agents make, and how to avoid them.

#1
THINKING YOU HAVE TO WORK WITH EVERYBODY

You don't. As Floyd loved to say, "You can't get them all. You don't want them all. Even if you got them all you couldn't help them all, so stop trying. Just work with your clients – those are the people who will do things your way and not fight you." When you're just getting started or trying to get restarted, you may think you have to take whoever you can get. The earlier you learn to be selective about who you say yes to, the longer you will last in this business.

One of the most important decisions you make every day is who and what to devote time to. Your time is irreplaceable and can't be saved, it can only be invested. The happiest Realtors® I know have clearly identified who their ideal clients are because they know that's who they work best with. They have criteria and standards the client must meet, and procedures to weed out those they cannot honestly and comfortably serve.

"The higher your standards, the longer the line will be to get in."

#2
WORKING OUT OF BALANCE FOR TOO LONG.

Most of us are out of balance somewhere in our lives at any given time, but success in real estate is not incompatible with a family life. It may just seem that way, especially if you don't put guardrails in place.

To build and maintain your "home court advantage" (the support and encouragement of those you love), schedule vacations with them in advance. They need a light at the end of tunnel, and they will live out of balance without you as long as they know for how long and what's in it for them.

Schedule LFT's. (See chapter 4.) Show up for your Look Forward To's. Treat them with the same importance as a listing appointment. They are the first thing to get blocked out on your weekly activity plan.

No question you are busy, and your hours are not always your choice, but let the people you care most about know what they can absolutely count on you for. We call them "countables." If you know for a fact that you can be home by 7, tell them you will be home by 8 for sure. Leave yourself a little room for error and you'll rarely disappoint your loved ones.

And finally, "hang it on the hook." When you get home at the end of the day, be at home. Leave real estate outside. There is no benefit to your loved ones hearing you complain about work when you are at home with them. Just as there is no benefit to you complaining to the people you work with about what's going on back home. Learn to separate business and personal time, or eventually you will pay a high price.

#3
BUYING LEADS

Think time, money and effort. Buying leads takes very little time or effort. That's the good news. The bad news is that it takes the most money, and with little or no guarantee of quality. It also creates dependence on sources that come and go. When you are getting started or restarted you probably have more time and energy than you have money. Invest in yourself and your education before you invest in anything else.

The skill of prospecting for your own leads has a lot in common with working out and building muscle. Once you stop working out, muscles have a tendency to weaken, and it's the same with prospecting.

Build your Book of Business. Hold open house. Do just listed and just sold canvassing. Prospect for listings in neighborhoods where your buyers want to buy. Supplement all this with social media groups and connections. Call on For Sale By Owners, expired and cancelled and withdrawn listings. And always be on the lookout for signs of homeowners who are thinking of moving, or who might have to sell – garage sales, home improvement crews, vacant or distressed properties, for rent signs, etc.

#4
NOT GETTING FACE-TO-FACE

Technology has made it possible to do almost everything remotely without human contact. It's quicker and easier, but are we missing something? Yes. Human contact, the basis for close personal relationships. And we also miss voice inflection, facial expression, body language and personality.

All of which is fine if you only want a transaction-based business and to eliminate the possibility of repeat and referral business.

Selling is a contact sport. Without being physically present, how do you detect buying signs while showing a house? Or build rapport while qualifying a seller? Or control what your clients see and hear, and in what order, when presenting an offer?

Take full advantage of the efficiency that technology

provides, but not at the expense of the sensory input of human contact. Rule of Thumb: "Always negotiate money face-to-face."

#5
BRAGGING ON SOCIAL MEDIA

This is Coach Kyle Draper's area of expertise, so while I don't claim to be an expert on social media, Kyle created a huge awareness around this for our audience at The Business Breakthrough. When you look at what most agents post on social media, you see awards and new listings and happy buyers with their new home, and it looks like all real estate agents are millionaires and this job is a piece of cake. It also looks like real estate is all we are and all we do.

Social media can be social and fun and relational, and it can reveal you as a whole person for your clients. Bragging about your awards (Did you know the average person sees "Million Dollar Producer" and thinks you made a million dollars?) is a turn-off, and gives only a one-sided picture of who you are.

Instead of bragging, engage with your people. Share their posts. Comment on their posts. DM them. And be a real person for them instead.

Commit that you will think differently from those who fail. Decide to take action and avoid making any of these mistakes.

"An ounce of prevention is worth a pound of cure."

CHAPTER 7:
It's Not The Calls You Make. It's That You Make The Calls.

There is nothing more important than keeping in touch with the people you know, even if it's just to tell them you have nothing to tell them, because if you are asking for business every time you call them, eventually they will stop taking your call.

By calls, we mean any form of contact or conversation. In other words, it's not as important how you keep in touch as it is that you keep in touch.

This rule of thumb also applies to keeping in touch with people you don't know and who don't know you. In other words, prospecting, which is the hardest thing to make yourself do consistently.

In all my years of training and coaching I have asked thousands of real estate agents why they were attracted to the business. The four most common reasons I have heard:
1. I get to be my own boss and make my own hours.
2. There is no ceiling on my income.
3. I love helping people.
4. I love houses.

Guess what I have never heard anyone say? I love prospecting! Nobody loves prospecting, but it is the only way to get the good stuff. When you make calls, good things happen. When you don't make calls, nothing happens.

Not only is making calls the secret to success, it's also one of the all-time great slump busters. Whether you are heading for a slump, or you're in a slump, or you're trying to get out of a slump, taking positive action by making the calls you don't want to make will always get you headed in a better direction.

When you make the calls, you feel better, and since most salespeople are emotional producers, when we feel good we are more productive. When we feel good we attract business to us because we look better, sound better and sell better.

Let's go back to the #1 reason people get into real estate – I get to be my own boss. That is the essence of being an independent contractor, and the best thing about real estate. It's also the worst thing about real estate, because in order to succeed you have to be your own boss. And what kind of boss are you?

How do you make yourself make more calls? I want you to write this answer down. Are you ready? Here it is. You can't. If you could, you would already be making more calls. But there is a way to make it easier. Get a partner, or partners with whom to prospect. *(See Chapter 8.)*

Prospecting is a numbers game. So is baseball. Professional ballplayers miss the ball more often than they hit it. In fact, the player with the highest career average, Ty Cobb, hit .366 which means he hit one in three, and "failed" two out of three times at bat. That's why baseball is known as a game of failure. Prospecting is also a game of failure. You will hear "No" way more often than you will hear "Yes."

ROGER AND THE LAW OF AVERAGES

Our friend, Roger, invites us to a unique charity event he holds twice a year to benefit the Carmelite Sisters of Los Angeles. When we first arrived at his home we were surprised to find a full-size Las Vegas style craps table in his family room. Roger is a dice game enthusiast with a mathematician's brain. He tracks every roll of the dice on a giant white board and can spot patterns and trends in the numbers. Every once in a while, he will advise all the players to take their bets down because it's time for a 7 to show up. And within a roll or two he is invariably right. Roger understands the law of averages.

MARY AND THE BOXES

Early in her sales career my wife, Mary was given a prospecting sheet with 100 boxes, 99 of them were labeled no, and just was one labeled yes. For every contact made she was instructed to X out either a no box or a yes box, depending on the prospect's response. She never once had to X out all 99 boxes of no before she got to a yes, and learned some very valuable lessons.

First, the only way to get better at prospecting is to do it a lot. Repetition is the mother of skill.

And the second lesson was this: "Anything worth doing well is worth doing poorly until you get it right."

Maybe the most important lesson of all, though, is that it never takes as many calls as you think it might to get to a yes. Persistence pays off when you let the law of averages work for you.

CHAPTER 8:
How To Make Yourself Make More Calls With The 5-90-10 System

Our founder (Floyd Wickman) built a very successful real estate career with cold calling as his primary prospecting method. Every Saturday he would arrive at the office by 8:30 AM and select a list of streets to cold call from the reverse directory, then clear off his desk, grab a cup of coffee and start dialing by 9:00. He would keep dialing until he scheduled 5 listing appointments for the coming week. And the key word is until. With this prospecting routine he produced an average of 86 listings a year for 7 years. That's over 600 listings!

When he created the famous Sweathogs program the assignment every student was required to do for the

Rethink Everything

first four weeks was the following: Go to office. 9:00 AM. Three mornings a week. Sit at desk. Open criss-cross directory. Pick street quick. Start at the bottom and cold call until you schedule a listing appointment. We called it 4 Weeks of Pain, and it created a lot of successful real estate agents.

One of the most important discoveries we made after hundreds of programs was that when a group of agents show up at the office by 9:00 AM and start prospecting together, they stick with it longer. They make more calls, have more conversations and schedule more appointments than they ever could as individuals working alone. We also discovered that when an office has only one or two agents in the program, they find this assignment incredibly difficult.

The camaraderie, the accountabililty, the shared misery and the shared celebration of success, the competitive juices stirred by group prospecting – all of these ingredients changed everything.

The Do Not Call Registry and the disappearance of home telephones made cold calling all but obsolete, and as the program evolved, the prospecting assignment changed to: Schedule and complete three 90 minute blocks of prospecting time each week. But something was missing, and I bet you can guess what it was.

Mary and I were in an accountability/mentor group with other trainers who prospected for appointments. We would schedule prospecting time together, and check in with each other before and after our calling sessions. Mary called it 5-90-10. 5 minute check-in to share who we were calling and what approach we were using, followed by 90 minutes of "smiling and dialing" and then a 10 minute check-in to report #'s dialed, conversations and results. When we added 5-90-10 to the program, it worked like magic, because it had so many of the ingredients of the group cold calling from Sweathogs.

Our students have been able to make themselves make more calls because they schedule prospecting time with a buddy, and treat it like an appointment. When you know someone else is counting on you, you show up and dial.

The most productive agents I know are consistently doing five 5-90-10 sessions a week, Monday through Friday. And they use a video app to connect for the first 5 minutes, but leave it on mute for the 90 minutes of phone prospecting so they can see each other! Talk about accountability!

5-90-10 has become so popular we wrote a song about it. Here are the lyrics *(sung to the tune of 'Sweet Caroline')*.

Rethink Everything

Where it began
'Twas in the mind of Mary
This great idea just came along
Day after day
Prospecting was such a bummer
Now thanks to her we're growing strong

Hands
Dialing hands
Reaching out
Calling me
Calling you

5 - 90 - 10
Calling never felt so good
I've been inclined
To believe it never would
But now I

I call up my friend
And it don't seem so lonely
Calling is easier with two

And when I hurt
Hurting runs off my shoulders
Knowing that you're calling, too

One
Dialing one
Reaching out
Calling me
Calling you

5 - 90 - 10
calling never felt so good
I've been inclined
To believe it never would

5 - 90 - 10
calling never felt so good
I've been inclined
To believe it never would

You get to choose who you're going to call. Past Clients, Expireds, FSBOs, old leads or old fashioned "cold" calling. It's not the calls you make. It's that you make the calls. And 5-90-10 is the secret to having enough conversations consistently so you can build your business.

Rethink Everything

CHAPTER 9:
How To Generate Your Own Leads Without Having To Pay For Them

There are essentially four ways to generate listing leads: pray for them, pay for them, make contacts with people you know and make contacts with people you don't know. Let's take them one at a time.

#1
PRAY FOR THEM

Never underestimate the power of prayer, divine intervention, telling the Universe to provide what you want, and visualizing prosperity and abundance with gratitude. In The Science Of Getting Rich, author Wallace D. Wattles wrote in 1911, "There is a thinking stuff from which all things are made and which, in its' original state, permeates, penetrates and fills the interspaces of the Universe. A thought, in this substance, produces the thing that is imaged by the thought." The most current research in quantum physics agrees with this principle. There is an unimaginably vast abundance available to all of us. Or as Reverend Edwene Gaines put it in her book, *The Four Spiritual Laws Of Prosperity*, "I have a very rich Father." I hope all that is not too esoteric for you, so let's continue.

#2
PAY FOR THEM

In a word, don't. But if you are at your wit's end and see no other way, limit yourself to those services you don't pay for up front, but pay a modest referral fee at closing; ask for Seller leads only; and only if the leads are exclusive to you. Google can show you which pay-for-leads services meet those criteria.

#3 & #4
MAKE CONTACTS WITH PEOPLE YOU KNOW AND PEOPLE YOU DON'T KNOW

In other words, generate your own leads. This is the most reliable, most controllable and, ultimately, the most sustainable method. There is a formula for making this work: buy in, set a goal, make a commitment, and do the basics.

Buy in to the fact that listings are the name of the game (see Chapter 2). Set a goal (How much do you want to earn? Why? Then, calculate how many listings you need to earn it. To get them, how many appointments do you need to attend? From there, how many leads do you need to land those appointments?) Goals need to be specific, measurable, with a deadline, and something that you want for you. Make a commitment. And what is commitment? Do or die. Wholehearted. I'm in. Tell everyone. Burn your bridges.

And finally, do the basics until they become a habit. ***Mine your Book of Business*** (the people you know and they people they know – see Chapter 4). Then pursue the traditional and non-traditional sources of leads, including:
- For Sale By Owners
- Expired, cancelled and withdrawn listings
- Just listed and just sold canvassing
- Open house
- Your network of retiring or limited service agents
- Geographic farming
- Social media groups
- Probate
- Pre-foreclosure and lis pendens
- Distressed and vacant properties
- Divorce
- Seniors
- Investors
- Builders
- Property managers
- Multi-family units
- Financial advisors, just to name a few…
- *and a few more...*

REGISTER AS A BUYER ON ZILLOW/TRULIA

Use your (free) Gmail address and request properties "not listed with a broker." Local For Sale By Owners contact information will appear in your inbox daily.

GOOGLE MAPPING

Visit local businesses and do a panoramic view of the exterior. Pin to the map and watch your search results climb!

HOST A CLIENT APPRECIATION EVENT

Support a local business by hiring them to cater your event, for example, an ice cream truck, a food truck, or a shredder. Hire out a local movie theater or bowling alley. Get your vendor partners to help underwrite costs. Invite selected clients to breakfast, lunch or dinner.

HOLD A CONTEST TO GENERATE 5 STAR REVIEWS

For each review, your clients are entered into a drawing for a gift of your choice (like a Yeti cooler). Offer double entries into the drawing for any 5 Star reviews!

RESEARCH RECENT LISTING AND SELLING ACTIVITY AND CHECK IN WITH EVERYONE YOU KNOW

Ask them to guess what's happening in real estate these days. They will be surprised with the good news that homes are being listed and sold; and that prices continue to rise, building their equity.

IT'S TIME TO INVITE THE PUBLIC TO FIRST TIME BUYER SEMINARS AGAIN

You can also host seller seminars and promote them with: How To Cash In Your Equity And Never Be Homeless, and How To Avoid Having To Move Twice. Have your broker or manager or vendor partner introduce you. Do your agency presentation for buyers, and your Buy/Sell Analysis presentation for sellers.

FOR RENT BY OWNERS

Contact property owner/landlords looking for tenants and offer to show them how much equity they have built.

HANDWRITE THANK YOU NOTES

Send one to every person you have a "positive conversation" with. One note per day five days a week to people in your Book of Business translates to everyone in your Book of Business receiving a personal note from you every year.

PROSPECT FOR LISTINGS WHILE PROPERTY SEARCHING FOR YOUR BUYERS

Once your buyer identifies the area and the type of home they are looking for, offer to door knock homes in that area until you find one for them. Tell each homeowner that you have a pre-approved buyer looking specifically in the neighborhood, and the promise you have made to the buyer to knock every door. And always ask, "Who's your Realtor?" If they say they don't have one, offer to apply for the job.

USE THE REFERRAL LEAD GENERATOR

That's our step-by-step prospecting track that uses your own words, to connect with your Book of Business (your 200 best repeat and referral business sources). Keep in touch with the people you know and get voice-to-voice at least three times a year. When you mail something monthly and follow up with a call, you double the effectiveness of your mailing. When you also get face-to-face once a year, you triple the effectiveness of your mailing and calling.

Generating your own leads is not only possible, it's profitable. You just read a long list of lead-generation possibilities. You don't have to do all of them. So, which ones will you commit to doing? When? Remember, it's what you do when you don't have to that determines what you will be when you can no longer help it.

CHAPTER 10:
How To Convert Leads Into Appointments

If you have all the leads you want, but you can't convert them into face-to-face appointments, they won't do you much good. Don't blame the leads. It's not their fault.

As Zig Ziglar famously said, *"When one finger is pointing at the excuse, three times as many are pointing back at the solution."* Instead of blaming the leads, get better at converting them into appointments. Let me introduce you to a system we teach our students that will take your conversion rate from hit or miss to bull's eye! It's a sales dialogue track called **The Lead To Appointment Converter.**

A dialogue track is different from a script. It is a process using your own words, instead of words someone else (or some thing else) wrote, but following a step-by-step approach. We use the term HOT BUTTON to describe a fair trade. You want an appointment, and you will get it by giving them something they want. What do they want? Information. Education. Advice. Something that will further their cause of buying or selling. It's fair. It's a trade.

A HOT BUTTON is an idea converted into a visual and given a name. The most common HOT BUTTON offered to Sellers as a fair trade is a current market analysis. Having a variety of HOT BUTTONS to offer will help you get more appointments and signatures. A list of possible HOT BUTTONS and their uses can be found at the end of this chapter.

> "The actual words you use are not as important as what you accomplish one step at a time."

Before we dive into the dialogue track, let's pretend you have been referred to a prospect by someone they know. Begin your conversation by finding out if you have been validated by the referring source.

Mr. Smith?

My name is Mike Pallin, and I'm with On Track Real Estate. I was speaking with your niece, Jennifer, and she mentioned that you folks are thinking of selling. She asked me to give you a call and I promised that I would. Have you heard from Jennifer?

Did she have good things to say about me?

That's great to hear. So, you are thinking of selling?

Validated and referred prospects are the most easily converted.

HERE IS THE
LEAD TO APPOINTMENT CONVERTER

STEP 1.
Find the HOT BUTTON by asking open-ended questions and listening for what they might be missing that you could provide.

EXAMPLE
So where are you thinking of moving to?
When would you like to be there?
What kind of home are you looking for?
Who is helping you find it?
When was the last time you had a current market analysis done on your home?
Where do you generally go to for real estate advice?

STEP 2.

Push the HOT BUTTON by describing the HOT BUTTON with a benefit to them and a drawback without it, and asking if they would be interested in hearing more about it.

EXAMPLE

Are you familiar with a Highest Price Analysis?

That's an overview of the current market including homes for sale right now – so that we know what the competition is asking; homes that have sold recently – so that we know what buyers are willing to pay; and homes that were on the market but didn't sell – so that we know what buyers are not willing to pay. It will help us determine the highest price you can ask without leaving money on the table.

Would something like that be of value to you?

STEP 3.

Propose a Get-Together. Keep it low key and pressure free vs "scheduling an appointment."

EXAMPLE

As long as that would be of interest, let's find a time when I can stop by and take a look at your house, and while I'm there, I'll go over the Highest Price Analysis with you. That way, at least you'll have all the information about pricing at your fingertips. I could stop by this afternoon at say 4:30, or would this evening be better for you?

If they say yes, you can skip the next four steps. Pre-qualify the appointment to make sure it's "gettable," including:
a. all the decision makers will be present
b. they will set aside enough time for you to do your full listing presentation
c. you have enough information about the property to do a ballpark market analysis
d. you have some idea of what they think the property is worth

If they don't say yes, but instead give you a reason not to get together now (which we call a hesitation) proceed to the next steps.

STEP 4.
Handle the hesitation. Investigate their reasons and offer another HOT BUTTON.

EXAMPLE
You probably have a good reason for feeling that way. Do you mind if I ask what it is?

If you knew that by waiting for _____, you might not be able to move on time, would you consider getting together with me now?

Are you familiar with the Real Estate Timing Analysis?

It's a bird's eye view of the time frames it currently takes a seller to get their house on the market, get it sold, get their money and move. It will help you time the move to get the best price and avoid having to postpone your move.

Would something like that be of value to you?

STEP 5.
Propose a Get-Together.

EXAMPLE

As long as that would be of interest, let's find a time when I can stop by and take a look at your house, and while I'm there, we'll go over the Timing Analysis. That way, at least you'll have all the information about timing at your fingertips. I could stop by this afternoon at say 4:30, or would this evening be better for you?

If they say yes, skip the next two steps and pre-qualify the appointment.

If they give you another hesitation (for example: we want to fix it up first) go to Steps 6 & 7.

STEP 6.
Handle the hesitation.

EXAMPLE
You probably have a good reason for feeling that way. Do you mind if I ask what it is?

If you knew that by fixing it up first, you might be costing yourself a small fortune, and I could show you how to save it, would you consider getting together with me now?

Are you familiar with the Financial Risk Analysis?

It's a survey of the factors that increase the value and marketability of a home. It will help you make decisions that will protect your equity and maximize your net proceeds, and avoid making improvements that cost a lot but don't return dollar for dollar.

Would something like that be of value to you?

STEP 7.
Propose a Get-Together.

EXAMPLE
Since that would be of interest, let's find a time when I can stop by and take a look at your house, and while I'm there, we'll go over the

Financial Risk Analysis. That way, at least you'll have all the information to make a decision about fixing it up at your fingertips. I could stop by this afternoon at say 4:30, or would this evening be better for you?

Notice that you ask for the get-together three times. If you have only one HOT BUTTON to offer that's not possible, so have enough to "close three times."

If you will build the habit of always asking for what you want three times, never any more, just never any less, you will almost always be able to get what you want without pushing people.

Remember the *"examples"* above are just that. You don't have to memorize them. You certainly don't read them while you're on the phone with a prospect. You use your words. You be you. Be conversational. Smile and have fun with them. When you do, and you follow the track, you'll convert more leads to appointments. And that's what it's all about.

HOT BUTTONS

- Highest Price Analysis
- Timing Analysis
- Financial Risk Analysis
- Marketability Checklist
  A list of factors that cause a house to either sell or not sell (especially useful for expired listings)
- Trends Analysis
  An overview of year-over-year market trends, including inventory levels, sales activity, days on market, median prices, and price per square foot
- Buy/Sell Analysis
  A comparison of the effects of selling before you buy vs buying before you sell
- Pro/Con Analysis
  A traditionasl decision-making tool for weighing the merits of key factors that influence a sale (especially useful when asked to discount your commission)
- Comparison Shopping Analysis
  A side-by-side comparison of marketing services and market share facts
- Sellers Information Package
  A sample package of all the forms and procedures needed to sell and close
- Buyers Information Package
  A sample package of all the forms and procedures needed to buy and close

Rethink Everything

CHAPTER 11:
The Pricing Presentation

WHEN TO PRESENT PRICE

When you present price on a listing appointment is just as important as how you present price. Often, the seller will ask the agent over the phone what they think the price or price range might be. Sometimes they ask right when the agent walks in the door. Sellers frequently greet agents at the door and offer a tour right away, during which they will say "So, what do you think it's worth?" In each of these cases, answering with a number is the wrong thing to say. Instead, you are going to set it aside so that you stop losing listings that you want to take.

Setting it aside is easy. You simply say, "Oh, we're going to cover that when we get back to the kitchen table." Or you may say, "I brought along all that information, and we'll go through it right after this tour."

The most consistently successful agents do not present price until they have asked for the listing subject to agree on a price. This is called a trial close and there is a sound selling principle behind it. If the seller doesn't express confidence that you can get the job done, your opinion about price is irrelevant. Decide right now that you will not give them a number before you have given your presentation and they are impressed!

Here are some examples of a trial close you could use after you've shown the seller your marketing plan and sold them on you:

> *"Let's pretend we put our heads together and come up with a price we both can live with, what else would you need to see or hear to be comfortable letting me handle your listing?"*

> *"Based on everything you've seen and heard tonight, if we could agree on a price, would there be anything preventing you from hiring me?"*

And how do you get to this point?
- Ring the bell, and then…
- Smile.
- Pay them a compliment.
- Take them to the kitchen table.
- Break the ice.
- Get their permission to follow your agenda.
- Ask your qualifying questions.
- Look at the house.
- Go back to the kitchen table.
- Show them your marketing plan and value proposition.
- Trial close for the listing subject to agreeing on price.

HOW TO PRESENT PRICE

Most agents think that pricing consists of showing comparables to the seller; that simply by comparing the subject home to similar properties it will be clear to the seller what the right price should be. Then they wonder why their prospects are confused and why the pricing discussion has turned into an argument. Remember instead to KISS, Keep It Simple Salesperson.

Of course you should do your market research and prepare a report, but you will not show it unless and until you have to. Begin instead with an explanation of price that every seller can relate to. Here's an example.

"As you know, there are three prices on every house. The first price is wholesale, or what a typical investor would pay to resell it and make a profit. (Show them what investors are paying for similar properties by writing down a dollar amount.)

The second price is retail, also known as market price, or what a typical buyer would pay to live here. (Show them market price based on your research of comparables and inspection of condition by writing down the price you think it will sell for. Be honest.)

The third price on every house is your list price, and that will be determined by how much time you have. May I show you how most successful sellers choose their list price?"

THE PRICE TIME PYRAMID

$210,000 — Immediately

$300,000 — February 24

So, when do you want your money?

This diagram illustrates the relationship between time and price. Up at the very top is the investor or wholesale price, which would take the shortest amount of time, usually at most a day or two and all cash.

Down at the bottom is the market price, which would take market time (average days on market from your MLS research), and which would mean you would move somewhere on or about this date. (Show probable moving date.)

If they ask how you came up with the market price, then and only then will you show them your market analysis. Your research into price might also include year-over-year data on sales activity, mortgage rates, absorption rates, days on market, median sales price and price per square foot.

Once the seller has seen how you came up with the price you recommend, ask this question:

"How soon do you need your money?

Based on your preferred timing, I recommend a list price of ($_____). Let's see what that would net you and see if you could live with that, fair enough?"

The key concept is to connect the price to their time frame, and then convert the price to a net figure as soon as possible. If they want to ask for more than market price, show them how much longer it will probably take to sell. You can base this future date on recent appreciation rates. The question is not whether they can get what they want for their home. The question is can they wait long enough for it to be worth that much?

This is a pricing presentation that works and is timeless. It's always true if you base it on current data and listen to the seller's timing goal. Every listing will sell at the right price, and every listing will sell if it's on the market long enough.

If you don't think that's true, take a house built in 1985 and find out the sales history. You will see that over time, it has increased in value. Imagine it's 2005, and the seller wants a 2030 price. Could they get it? Yes. If they waited until 2030. (You may not even want that listing!). You never again have to tell people they cannot get their too-high price. They can! They will just have to wait longer. If they don't want to wait that long, they usually get more reasonable. It's your job to teach them how the price they choose is related to how long it takes to sell and that will determine when they get to move. ***Time is money.***

5-Steps For Handling Hesitation
1. CUSHION IT
2. QUESTION IT
3. ISOLATE IT
4. HANDLE IT
5. CLOSE

CHAPTER 12:
How To Handle Hesitations

Hesitations are also known as objections, stalls, excuses, conditions, roadblocks, challenges, obstacles… in essence they boil down to whatever the prospect says when they don't feel they should say yes. In other words, it's not a no, it's just not a yes. Yet.

There are three times when you should handle a prospect's hesitation: never, later and when it arises.

Let's start with never. Some hesitations can be ignored in the moment. If I'm showing a home and the buyer says, "This room's too small," there's nothing I can say right now or ever that will make it larger. Trying to handle this hesitation is pointless unless it comes up again.

Some hesitations should be set aside until the time is right. A perfect example is the listing prospect who wants you to quote a commission over the phone before agreeing to an appointment. You don't know if you even want their listing, or if you can sell it, or if you can agree on a price. Set it aside. "Commissions are negotiable. I'm willing to work for whatever commission you and I can agree on, fair enough?"

And then there are hesitations that need to be handled in order to get a decision or a signature. Your prospect isn't saying no, they're just saying not yet.

In sales, as in life, no means no. It is not an invitation for you to probe and push. Thank you, next. Move along.

But anything other than a clear and unequivocal no should at least be explored. There is a chance you have left important questions unanswered. In fact, there are as many possibilities in any given sales situation as there are people.

We believe that if you have told your prospects everything they need to know to make a decision, and they have told you everything you need to know to make a decision, you deserve a decision. You and your prospects deserve a resolution, because anything other than a yes or a no is just a decision not to decide.

Unfortunately most people are indecisive and hesitant to commit, so they often need leadership from you to make a decision. Professional salespeople don't ever have to push if they know how to lead.

We teach a 5 step process for handling hesitations that has helped thousands of agents help millions of clients make decisions. That is actually part of the job description of a professional salesperson: to help your clients make decisions which, left up to themselves, they wouldn't ordinarily be able to make, but will thank you for later.

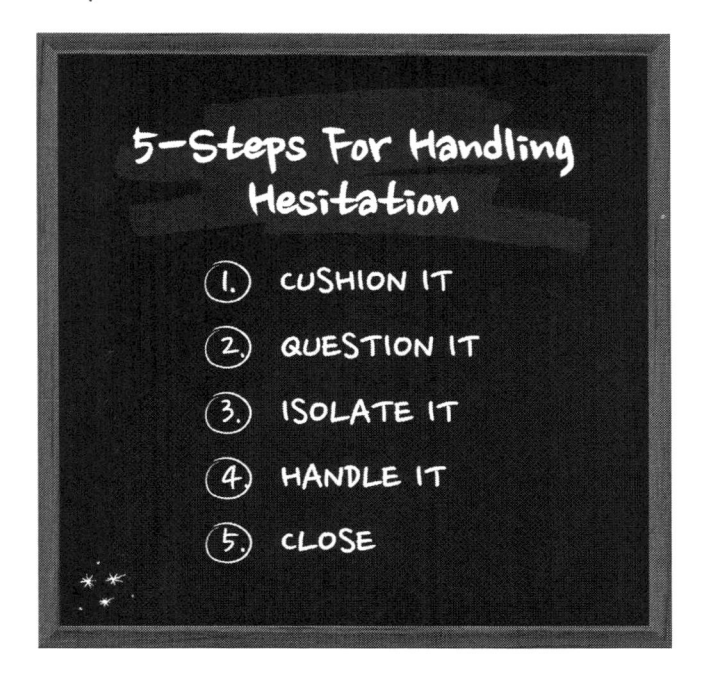

5-Steps For Handling Hesitation

1. CUSHION IT
2. QUESTION IT
3. ISOLATE IT
4. HANDLE IT
5. CLOSE

STEP 1 - CUSHION IT
Make a statement that shows you're not going to argue.

STEP 2 - QUESTION IT
Ask open-ended questions to keep your prospect talking about their thoughts and feelings.

STEP 3 - ISOLATE IT
Make sure this hesitation is the only one holding them back.

STEP 4 - HANDLE IT
Show them something relevant to their situation. A visual and a few well-chosen words are always more persuasive than just the words.

STEP 5 - CLOSE
Ask for agreement, and assume what you said and showed them worked to change their thoughts and feelings.

In this example, the prospects say they will list with you but only if you are willing to price it above the figure you advised.

They say:
"We know you recommend listing at $699,000, but we want to at least try $799,000 first."

You say:
STEP 1

> Thank you for bringing that up.

STEP 2

> I'm sure you have a good reason for feeling that way. Do you mind if I ask what it is?

> "We want to have some negotiating room in case we get an offer."

> OK, I totally understand. Just out of curiosity, if you got an offer at the list price we talked about earlier, and the cash figure it would net, would you accept it?

> "Well, yeah, of course."

> How important is being able to stick to the timetable you mentioned?

>> "That's very important. We have to move by then."

> So, you're just wanting to speculate a bit on a higher price?

>> "Yes, that's it."

> No problem. How long would you be willing to stay at that price if we get no offers or showings?

>> "At least a couple weeks."

> Right. Let me see if I understand what you're thinking. You're willing to accept an offer that gets you the net figure you need, but you want to try a higher asking price for at least a couple of weeks just to see if we can get it. Is that what you're thinking?

STEP 3

> So, is that the only thing preventing us from getting the ball rolling tonight?

> "Yes."

What if you knew that pricing it at the higher figure might jeopardize your ability to move on time. Would you be willing to consider an alternative strategy?

> "Yes."

STEP 4

Let me show you something that could prevent us from making a mistake. This chart tells us when the most showings occur on a new listing, and how quickly activity from buyers drops off after the first two weeks. That's pretty remarkable isn't it?

> "Oh, boy, I'll say."

You see, I'd rather see you take full advantage of the most activity and stand firm on your price, than never get any showings and miss your deadline for moving.

STEP 5

So, any other questions? Good, let's go back to the paragraph in the listing agreement we just left…

The good news is that there are only a few hesitations you need to handle, and they mostly boil down to one of the following:

We want to find one to buy before we list
We want to fix it up first
We want to wait until _____
We want to try it ourselves first
We want to try a higher price
We have a friend in the business
We want to talk to other agents
We want you to discount your commission
We don't want to pay a commission
You don't have enough experience

Receiving a hesitation or objection from your prospect when you ask for a signature at the end of a presentation isn't the end of the world, but it can be frustrating and surprising. Stay calm and trust the process. It's not step 1 that handles the hesitation, and it's not step 2, either. Or steps 3 or 4 or 5. It's the combination of all the steps followed in order that handles any hesitation.

CHAPTER 13:
Client Appreciation Events That Pay Off

Throughout this book you have been reading about building a Book of Business by implementing a Mail-Call-See marketing system. Mail (or send) your 200 best repeat and referral sources something every month, call them three times a year, and see them in person once a year.

Some of our graduates prefer dropping by for individual visits and delivering a poinsettia at holiday time, or tulip bulbs in spring. Some take individuals or groups to breakfast or lunch or dinner. Some have dinner parties. And some throw massive parties.

Rethink Everything

Laura rents a shredder right after tax season and invites them to her office for a free shredding. Bob hires an ice cream truck at the fire hall to benefit first responders, law enforcement and firefighters. Mary Anne runs a very successful coat drive every winter. Michelle offers pumpkin pies at Thanksgiving – place your order in advance and stop by Wednesday to pick up your pie. Mark runs an Easter egg hunt in the spring and a corn maze in the fall.

These events require planning on your marketing calendar and sticking to a budget, and the purpose is to have live, face-to-face human contact with your VIPs at least once a year. Mailing and calling doubles the effectiveness of your contacts. Adding a live event or contact creates permanent memorability.

Here is a case study of an annual client appreciation event that created an unforgettable experience, built lasting relationships, and literally paid for itself.

A CASE STUDY

Angie, one of my coaching students, holds an annual appreciation event for her past and present clients and their families and friends at a 48 lane bowling center. Her most recent event was held from 6PM to 9PM on a Thursday evening to avoid the weekend. She mailed out two sets of post card invitations, along with social media promotions on Facebook.

Over 300 people attended. The bowling center owner

is Angie's long-time client and donated his staff as well as alley time and shoes for all who participated. He said it's worth it to him to get that many people into his establishment on a weeknight. When he turned the lights down and activated the "Glow Bowl" enhancement, the whole room went "Ooooh!" and applauded.

Angie arranged a photo booth that printed each photo with her phone number on it, and also texted the photo to each person with a link to post on the Facebook event page. Magic Steve worked the room. All the kids were lined up for his balloon animals (and a crown for Angie) and his magic tricks. And her favorite lender and title company displayed their banners.

Once the bowling was underway, Angie visited each table for quality conversation time, to catch up on what's happening in everyone's lives, and answer the inevitable real estate questions.

COST BREAKDOWN
$400   Wait staff tips
$250   Kitchen staff tips
$350   Food
$375   Photo booth
$250   Magic Steve

Let's look at the ingredients that helped make this a very successful self-liquidating client appreciation event.

Rethink Everything

- Gratitude and appreciation
- Generosity to the wait and kitchen staffs
- Family friendly activities
- Fun activities that draw people
- A wow factor with the Glow Bowling
- Personal touch and conversation with each person attending
- Sponsors to offset costs
- Promoting a local business
- Memorializing the event on social media

And here's your host:

The best client appreciation events are meant to express gratitude to your clients, so they should come from your heart and your unique personality.

Make a commitment today to thank the people who make your business possible in person at least once a year. Figure out what you want to do, take out your marketing calendar and start planning.

Rethink Everything

CHAPTER 14:
Finding Off-Market Properties

There are basically two approaches to working with buyers – reactive and proactive. The reactive agents wait for MLS notifications that someone else has listed a property they can show to their buyer. When there is a super abundance of listings in your MLS to choose from, this might be the logical place to start, but that's not always the market we have, is it?

In an unbalanced market with a limited supply of listings, we have to do better than that. The end result of relying exclusively on the MLS to provide your selection has been feeding frenzy auctions, frustrated and disappointed buyers, and sellers with unrealistic expectations. There is a better way.

Proactive agents know that the perfect property for their buyer probably isn't on the market yet, and it may never be if they don't go out and find it first. Proactive agents understand that this is the job; this is how we fulfill our duty and responsibility to the client; and that this is how we can differentiate ourselves in a competitive environment.

The key is to look for homeowners who are [or might be] thinking of selling. Here are some places you can look for them:

FOR SALE BY OWNERS

The most obvious sign that someone is thinking of selling their home is a For Sale By Owner sign. Have you ever driven by a For Sale By Owner sign and not stopped? Relax. If no one is home, no one can holler at you. Leave your card with a note,

"Who is showing your home when you're not available? Call me. I can help. Let's get together."

If the owner is home, ask this question. *"Have you found a buyer yet?"* There are three possible responses you can hear. Yes, no or "Get off my lawn." Take your conversational cue from their answer.

EXPIRED, CANCELED & WITHDRAWN LISTINGS

"I noticed that your home was for sale recently and didn't sell. What were your plans if it had sold? Do you still want to sell?"

There are excellent fee services that will provide For Sale By Owner and expired listing contact information for you daily.

DOOR KNOCKING

Door knock in the neighborhoods where your buyers are looking and use the Specific Buyer Approach –

"I'm working for a couple who have specifically asked me to find them a home in this neighborhood. They are pre-approved for a mortgage and well qualified. I made them a promise that I will speak with every homeowner until I find them a place to live. So, have you even considered moving? Who do you know that might be? And who is your Realtor®?"

(BTW, check with Fair Housing guidelines on what information you can and cannot share about your buyers.)

PRIVATE NETWORK, COMING SOON & POCKET LISTINGS

Many of the agents in your office, company or agent network have been on listing appointments they didn't get, and know of sellers who haven't listed with anyone yet. Tell them about your buyers and ask for their help.

LIS PENDENS, PRE-FORECLOSURE AND REO (bank-owned properties)

Cultivate relationships with bank asset managers who are in the know. Show them that you are different from other agents by following up. Maybe they will ask you to do a BPO for them. Be willing to serve before you receive.

PROBATE ATTORNEYS AND ADMINISTRATORS

Consider checking the courthouse and county record sources. Befriend the people who work a 9am to 5pm shift there and build a relationship with them.

DIVORCE ATTORNEYS, COUNSELORS AND ARBITRATORS

Visit and build relationships with those who help people who need to sell.

BOLO

Be on the lookout as you travel in and around your market for these tell-tale signs.

- *For Rent By Owner*
- *Dumpster or POD in the front*
- *Garage/moving sales*
- *Signs of "deferred maintenance" such as unplowed driveway or unmowed lawn*
- *Contractor vehicles*
- *Landscapers at work*
- *Painters*
- *Shuttered and/or vacant homes*

When you see a sign, stop and investigate. Talk to the neighbors. Talk to the contractors at work. Check county records. Where do the tax bills go? Check forewarn.com. Send letters. Send video texts. Call. Stop by again. Follow up.

And finally, canvas around new listings and recent sales, even if you aren't the listing or selling agent involved. What if the listing agent or the buyer's agent is reactive and not reaching out to all the homeowners around recent activity? By the way, no matter how many times you may have heard that just listed and just sold canvassing pays off, it is still the exceptional agent that does it consistently.

Let me paraphrase a well-known saying, "Seek and you will find." Stop waiting and start seeking. When you are proactive, you are serving your buyers and they will not only be grateful, they will tell others how special you are.

Even if your search doesn't find them the right home, and they end up buying a property that someone else lists, you will meet people who want to sell. When your efforts impress those prospects, "leaving no stone unturned" will result in listings you wouldn't have gotten otherwise.

CHAPTER 15:
Train The Brain

"Floyd, if you're going to teach your students selling skills without working on character too, the selling skills won't last."

That statement from Zig Ziglar to Floyd Wickman became the hallmark of every platform and classroom message Floyd spoke after hearing his mentor's recommendation.

The human brain is elegant, complex, astonishing, magnificent and in many ways a total mystery. More is unknown than known about how the brain operates and affects our daily behavior, but one thing almost all the experts agree on is that your brain is a learning machine. We are, in other words, trainable.

When your brain is operating at peak efficiency, it is your greatest asset. When your brain is troubled, confused, distracted or overwhelmed, the brain can be your biggest problem. Have you ever had a day when you just couldn't seem to focus on anything? Have you ever felt consumed by worry?

We teach our students two techniques that you can adopt immediately to make a major difference in your productivity, focus and peace of mind. We call it "Train the Brain" but it's really training your mind. You'll want to implement both immediately. They are Morning Routine and Complete Your Circles.

MORNING ROUTINE

Our Master Salesperson Pledge (see the full text below) is an affirmation we repeat out loud each day. It originated from a life-changing moment when our founder was at a pivotal point in his life and career. His attitude was spiraling out of control into despair, but this caused him to skyrocket to the height of success. He was told,

> "Unless you change the way you are thinking, you are going to be out of the business. So, here's what I want you to repeat to yourself over and over, all day."

And as a result, he came to believe the phrase and believe in himself. But the impact didn't stop there. Floyd Wickman affected millions of lives because of his success. *Millions.*

What's in store for you? If you were to control your thinking, how many lives could you affect? By now, you're excited to hear the phrase, aren't you? But the real work comes when you take it and apply it to your morning routine….and then say it throughout the day.

This was the text of the affirmation Floyd was told to repeat:

> "I am a successful salesperson. As such, I will always be guided to do and say the things that contribute to my success. Anything that happens - happens in my best interest."

Where does this miraculous guidance come from? And how do you access it? The answers can be found in sticking to a morning routine.

Training the brain works best first thing in the day —before work begins, before any media or screens —first thing in your newly-rested mind. If you have family or chores before you can have privacy, delay your morning routine until you can have undisturbed quiet. ***Better yet, get up earlier.***

The ingredients of your new routine will be inspiration, meditation, visualization and/or recitation. Any one of them is effective. In combination, they can be miraculous.

INSPIRATION

Read or listen to something inspirational, uplifting and positive. Many of our students use Scripture for their inspiration. You could choose one of the classic sales books like Og Mandino's *The Greatest Salesman In The World* (the text is available on YouTube and read by the author). Or try reading *Think And Grow Rich* by Napoleon Hill. You choose. It doesn't have to be more than a few minutes, but it should inspire you.

MEDITATION

I majored in comparative religion as an undergraduate and graduate student and one of the most common ingredients of all faiths is a prescription for a daily period of quiet meditation. Whether you call it prayer or silence or just sitting quietly doing nothing, it is the practice of centering the self and listening for guidance. It becomes harder every day to hear that "still, small voice" as the world becomes noisier. Even a few minutes of quiet at the beginning of the day will help insulate you from the daily clamor for your attention.

The guidance you are listening for flows through your mind on the river of your thoughts. With practice you will become able to observe this "river" and to listen to the thoughts that guide you in choosing what you do and say for the rest of the day.

VISUALIZATION

Every great achievement of mankind began as a thought pictured in someone's mind. When you can see what you want clearly in your mind, you are more likely to be able to achieve it in your life. We require our students to set a goal and find a full color picture of the goal and carry it with them at all times. After the program, many of them create vision boards that guide their daily visualization sessions.

At the dawn of the personal development era in the early 1900's, Wallace D. Wattles wrote in his pamphlet, *The Science Of Getting Rich*,

> "There is a thinking stuff from which all things are made and which, in its original state, permeates, penetrates and fills the interspaces of the universe. A thought in this substance produces the thing that is imaged by the thought."

The most current beliefs in quantum physics about how the Universe works substantiates Mr. Wattles. It is no longer theory. It's fact. What you see (in your mind) is what you get in your world.

RECITATION

If you have ever been entertained by a hypnotist on stage, you have witnessed how suggestible the brain is. It will do what it is programmed to do. In the book *Psycho-Cybernetics*, Dr. Maxwell Maltz teaches us that the brain is a goal-striving mechanism. Give it a goal, and it will do everything in its power to hit it. It doesn't say *"that's impossible"* or *"that's not a positive goal"* – it just goes after the goal we give it. By repeating positive, first-person, present-tense affirmations you will train your brain to move you toward the person you want to become. The magic of affirmations is that you don't have to believe them for them to work. You just have to repeat them. Repetition is the gateway to growth and change.

Write out your own affirmation statements. Read them silently to yourself. Even better, read them aloud. Make a voice recording and listen to it daily.

> *"When you work on the inside,
> it shows on the outside."*

COMPLETE YOUR CIRCLES

Are you ready for the second technique that will give you peace of mind and focus? Here it is: complete your circles.

If psychologists could diagram the cause of nervous breakdowns it would look like a whole bunch of incomplete circles. Every time we start a task and leave it unfinished, every time we are interrupted mid-thought and leave something unresolved, we are creating an incomplete circle. These unfinished circles take up space in your brain, and when you have too many of them at once, they rob you of the ability to pay attention and stay on task.

So, here is RULE #1 about things on your To-Do List. If you start something, finish it, or else don't even start it. When you re-start something you have left unfinished you don't pick up where you left off. You usually have to go back to the beginning, remind yourself of what you were doing and thinking, and then start again. And that takes extra time. This has been robbing you of efficiency and focus. If you want to increase productivity, decide right now that if you start it, you will finish it. When beginning a big project, always start by breaking it into smaller pieces that can be done to completion.

And here is RULE #2. Begin your workday by taking out your To Do List and think. Ask yourself what your highest priorities are for that day. Call to mind your goal, and look at the tasks before you. What will get you closer to its achievement? Of all the things you could choose, select the top 5 most important things to do, write them down, and work on them first. Top producers consistently work high priority activities. Low and non-producers do not.

By now I hope you have made a commitment to get better and smarter and more skillful at listing and selling real estate. When you add the inspiration from a morning routine, and the discipline of working high priority activities, the sky is the limit!

I am a Master Salesperson

As such I am always guided to do and say the things that contribute to my success

EACH DAY I walk and talk like the Master Salesperson I am

EACH DAY my Core Values direct my activities

EACH DAY I take the steps that lead me closer to my goals

EACH DAY I accept adversities as friendly foes and learn from them

EACH DAY I perform with an air of confidence yet I show others that I care about them

EACH DAY when asked the secret of my success I gladly take the time to share

From this moment on, anything that happens – happens in my best interest, because

I am a Master Salesperson!

©The Floyd Wickman Team

CHAPTER 16:
Create Accountability

There are two kinds of accountability – *internal and external.*

My friend Dave was facing knee replacement surgery and asked his doctor if there was anything he could do to put off the need for surgery. The doctor told him to lose weight and that would take some of the pressure off.

On December 31st, Dave made a New Year's Resolution to lose 15 pounds. By March of the new year, he told me, "I only have 25 pounds more to lose. That's when I realized my weight loss plan wasn't working so well." Keep in mind, Dave is one of the most successful people in his field and has always been fastidious about his appearance. But self-motivation wasn't working.

So, Dave joined a weight loss program. Once a week he drove 30 minutes to meet his "coach" for a weigh in, consultation and pep talk. He ate what they told him to eat, when they told him to eat it and how much they told him to eat. In six weeks he lost all the weight he had gained on his own, plus all the original weight he had resolved to lose.

External accountability gets results by inspecting what is expected, and by measuring progress.

I remember having trouble getting my taxes done because I was engaging in all kinds of avoidance behavior and procrastination. In conversation with my best friend, John, I discovered he was having the same problem. So, we formed an accountability partnership. Once a week we worked on our taxes together. We scheduled 90 minutes each Wednesday from noon to 1:30 pm. At 11:55 am I called John and for five minutes we shared with each other what steps we were taking and what progress we wanted to make. Then we hung up and slogged through the process for 90 minutes. At 1:30 we reconnected and shared our successes and challenges. Eventually we both got our taxes completed, filed and paid.

External accountability removes excuses.

My wife will tell you that when we have company coming for dinner and she has all day to clean the house, it takes all day to clean the house. But when we have company coming for dinner in 30 minutes, she can clean the house in 30 minutes. This is because time expands. The longer you have to do something, the longer it takes.

External accountability creates deadlines and priorities.

When Mary and I created our coaching program we knew it had to include all the ingredients that made Floyd Wickman training so effective. We made sure it included accountability and teamwork, with mandatory assignments, and minimum standards. We built in tracking and reporting numbers, measuring progress to specific goals, sharing best practices, reminders of basic principles. We added support and encouragement, and collective brainstorming of problems. Since 2009, the agents we've coached have consistently achieved an average of 103% of their production goals.

If you want to succeed at anything, create accountability. If you happen to be one of the fortunate few who don't need accountability because you are totally self-motivated, how much more could you do if you put yourself in a position to stretch even further?

For more information about The Floyd Wickman Team's R Squared Coaching programs

Check out the other books
in the series

RETHINK EVERYTHING
YOU "KNOW" ABOUT SOCIAL MEDIA

KYLE DRAPER

RETHINK EVERYTHING
YOU 'KNOW' ABOUT BEING A NEXT GEN LOAN OFFICER

KYLE DRAPER
BRIAN VIEAUX